ACHIEVE LEVEL 4

ENGLISH Practice Questions

By **Richard Cooper**

RISING★STARS

Rising Stars UK Ltd., 22 Grafton Street, London W1S 4EX

www.risingstars-uk.com

All facts are correct at time of going to press.

This edition 2005
Reprinted 2006

Editorial: Tanya Solomons
Design: Ken Vail Graphic Design
Layout: Branford Graphics
Cover design: Burville Riley
Illustrations: Burville Riley, Beehive Illustration (Theresa Tibbets),
Graham-Cameron Illustration (Anthony Maher)

British Library Cataloguing in Publication Data

A CIP record for this book is available from the British Library.

ISBN 1-905056-03-6

Printed by Craft Print International Ltd, Singapore

The publisher and authors would like to thank the following for permission to use copyright material. Every effort has been made to contact copyright holders of material reproduced in this book. Any omissions will be rectified in subsequent printings if notice is given to the publisher.

p32 Charm School, © Anne Fine, David Higham Associates (Corgi Yearling); p34 The Magic Box from Cat Among the Pigeons by Kit Wright (Viking Kestrel, 1987), © Kit Wright 1984, 1987.

Contents

How to use this book   4

The National Tests   6

Section 1: Writing non-fiction   8

Section 2: Writing fiction   18

Section 3: Reading comprehension   28

Section 4: Spelling   40

Section 5: Punctuation   44

Section 6: Vocabulary   50

Section 7: Reviewing your work   54

Section 8: Handwriting   55

The answers can be found in a pull-out section in the middle of this book.

How to use this book

Practising non-fiction text features (pages 8 to 11)

(1) Description of the non-fiction text features including dos and don'ts.

(2) Practice questions to help you master these important features of writing.

Writing non-fiction (pages 12 to 17)

(1) **Definition** and **Purpose** – Helps you to understand what this type of writing is for and how it is used.

(2) **Text structure** – Flow chart that describes the key elements of the text type, in order.

(3) **Long tasks** – Practice questions so you can master this type of writing.

(4) **Short tasks** – Practice questions specially aimed at the **new** short tasks.

(5) **Tip** – Additional help to support all writers.

Writing fiction 1 (pages 18 to 21)

★ Introduction to classic story structure.

★ Also provides advice and practice questions so you can master the key features of fiction writing, including settings and character descriptions.

Writing fiction 2 (pages 22 to 27)

Useful planning grids for each genre of fiction and lots of independent writing tasks for you to complete.

Reading comprehension (pages 28 to 39)

1 **The text** – A range of texts are given, including fiction, non-fiction and poetry.

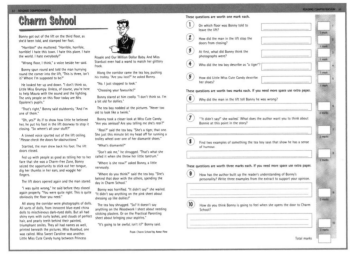

2 **The questions** – Comprehension questions that allow you to demonstrate your Level 4 skills. The number of marks available is given and there is space to write your answers.

Additional support

Spelling practice (pages 40 to 43)

These exercises are designed to give useful practice in the more difficult areas of spelling – plurals, tenses and common errors.

Punctuation (pages 44 to 49)

A range of exercises covering key Level 4 punctuation, includes work on the use of ellipses, dashes and semi-colons. It also includes a quick punctuation test.

Vocabulary (pages 50 to 53)

The vocabulary exercises focus on improving your writing by making sure that 'every word counts'. Each section has a brief explanation followed by exercises in developing and using a Level 4 vocabulary.

Reviewing your work and Handwriting (pages 54 to 55)

Supportive notes on how to review your writing continually.

The National Tests

Key Facts

★ The Key Stage 2 National Tests (or SATs) take place in the middle of May in Year 6. You will be tested on Maths, English and Science.

★ The tests take place in your school and will be marked by examiners – not your teacher!

★ You will get your results in July, two months after you take the tests.

★ Individual test scores are not made public but a school's combined scores are published in what are commonly known as league tables.

The English National Tests

You will take four tests in English. These are designed to test your Reading, Writing and Spelling. Your handwriting will be assessed through the Writing Tests.

Don't forget!

1) There is now one long and one short Writing Test (instead of two long ones).
2) There will be a new mark scheme for Writing.
3) Handwriting will be assessed in the long writing task – there is no separate handwriting test.

The Writing Tests

There are now two Writing Tests - one short (about 20 minutes) and one longer test (about 45 minutes). Remember to keep your handwriting neat for these tests.

The Short Writing Task is 20 minutes long. You will have some time to plan and space on the paper to make brief notes but remember that you only have 20 minutes to write your piece.

The Long Writing Task is 45 minutes long. You will have about 10 minutes to plan and there should be some space to write notes too. Remember you only have 45 minutes to complete the whole task!

Where to go to get help

Pages 8 to 27 are designed to help you succeed in the writing tests and include a variety of long and short tasks.

Pages 44 to 54 will help you to give 'voice' to your writing, sharpen up your punctuation and improve your grammar.

The Reading Test

There is one test to assess your reading comprehension. It will last about 1 hour. In this test you will be given a series of texts and an answer paper. You will be allowed to use the texts to answer the questions, so you won't need to memorise them.

Where to go to get help

Pages 28 to 39 give you practice in answering reading comprehension questions, which will help with the Reading Test.

The Spelling Test

There is one 15 minute Spelling Test. Your teacher will read a passage (or play a cassette with someone else reading the passage). You will have to write the words to complete the passage.

Where to go to get help

Pages 40 to 43 give you practice in spelling.

The Short Writing Task

Pages 22 to 27 give you an opportunity to practise elements of a complete narrative. You can use these activities to practise writing for 20 minutes. Set your clock and start writing!

Pages 12 to 17 allow you to practise writing non-fiction pieces. You can vary the time you use between 20 and 45 minutes to give you practice in each test.

Practising non-fiction text features

The passive voice or impersonal writing

Re-write these paragraphs using a more formal tone.

1 You mustn't take your eye off the ball when playing football. If you want to win the game, you need to force an opening by hitting the ball really hard so your opponent has little time to react.

_____

_____

_____

_____

_____

2 Petrol-guzzling cars are damaging to the environment. I read an article in the paper about how the fumes from big cars, like my dad's, are causing the quality of air in cities to fall.

_____

_____

_____

_____

_____

3 Making an omelette is fun. The best bit is breaking the eggs into the bowl. If you're really clever you can do it with one hand, but if you're not it can make a real mess!

_____

_____

_____

_____

Formal descriptions

Re-write these sentences using a more formal description.

1 Fast food has almost become a disease within our society. Too many people are eating fatty, unhealthy, nutrition-free products. Good, wholesome fresh fruit and crunchy vegetables are much better for you.

2 Looking into the sad, lost eyes of an abandoned puppy, you will realise how much that puppy's suffering could affect even the hardest of hearts.

3 Just looking at the wet, squishy clay is enough to make me want to grab a big sloppy handful and play with it on the kitchen table. Of course, it would make a horrendous mess.

4 As Rosie approached the rusting gates of the old manor house, she felt a warm tingle of anticipation run down her spine. Would the dashing young man be there to meet her as he'd promised just hours before?

Simple present tense

Re-write these sentences in the simple present tense.

1 The sunny weather was the main reason people went to Spain for their holidays.

2 Motor racing has been a very dangerous sport to take part in. Accidents occurred often.

3 The Derby was a very famous horse race. It always attracted huge crowds of spectators.

4 Gardening was one of the most popular pastimes in this country. Each season gave the gardener something to think about.

5 The train was late because of the dreadful weather we had yesterday.

6 We washed up the dirty plates that were lying in the sink.

7 The test was hard but I did my best.

Connectives

Complete these sentences using connectives. More than one connective fits each sentence. Choose the one that fits the best.

1 [_____], roll the dice.

[_____], move the counter along the board.

2 The bike went out of control [_____]

the tyres were flat. [_____], no one was seriously injured.

3 [_____] the flood, everyone returned to their

houses. [_____], some households were undamaged.

4 [_____] that's how the Romans became so successful.

[_____] what did the Romans ever do for us?

5 [_____] if you take out our policy we will give you a free

cuddly toy. [_____] we will give you the first month free.

6 [_____] due to your ridiculous behaviour, we are now banned

from playing football at lunchtime. [_____] we lost the final.

7 [_____], people say that skiing is dangerous,

[_____], skiers would say that they know the risks.

Persuasion

Definition
A persuasive text tries to make the reader think, do or buy something.

Purpose To persuade.

Text structure

① Identify the point of the text

② Reasons to support the point, organised into paragraphs

③ Summary of the key reasons

Long tasks

You will have 45 minutes for each long task. Remember to plan your writing before you start.

① Write a letter to the local council to persuade them that there is a real need in the area for an amusement park with free attractions for the under 12s.

② You have just opened a shop that sells beach toys, souvenirs, swimming costumes and sun hats. Unfortunately, you have just realised the town you're living in is 50 miles from the sea! Write an article to place in the local paper that will persuade people to come to your shop.

Short tasks

You will have 20 minutes for each short task. Remember to make sure you have enough time to complete the task.

① Design a poster that will persuade people that pulling funny faces in public is a bad idea.

② Write an advert to sell your bike, which was accidentally run over by a steamroller last week.

Instructions

Definition

Instructions tell a reader how to do, make or play something or how to get somewhere.

Purpose To instruct.

Text structure

1 Aim — This is the title and tells a reader what the instructions are about.

2 What you need — A list of the things that are needed to achieve the aim. These are listed in order of use.

3 What you do — A step-by-step chronological (time order) sequence of what to do to achieve the aim.

Long tasks

These are long writing tasks, so you have 45 minutes to plan, write and check your writing.

1 Your little sister wants to know how to play your favourite board game, "Cluedon't". However, the rules are missing from the box. Write out a set of rules to replace the ones that have been lost.

2 Imagine you are a top TV chef who is writing a recipe book to accompany your first series. Your most popular dish from the TV programme was "Bean Surprise". (Beans on toast with melted cheese and hot pepper chilli sauce.) Write the recipe for your new book!

Short tasks

These are short writing tasks, so you have 20 minutes to plan, write and check your writing.

1 You have a supply teacher for the day who has never been to your school before. Very kindly you offer to write down the structure of the day because your everyday teacher had to leave in a rush and didn't leave behind any instructions. You realise that the supply teacher will believe anything you happen to write!
You start with   *9.00 Register*
     9.05 Chewing gum testing. One packet per pupil.
     Continue!

2 You and your family are going on holiday leaving your pet dragon behind (he doesn't like flying). Luckily your rather nervous next-door neighbour has agreed to look after Smog while you are away. Leave some instructions for your neighbour on the best way to deal with Smog if he starts misbehaving.

Tip Instructions can be in the form of recipes, rules for playing a game, pictures or directions. Remember to think about the **purpose** of the writing!

Explanation

Definition

An explanation tells the reader how or why something works or happens. It can be about natural things, e.g. *How lakes are formed*, or about mechanical things, e.g. *How a telephone works*.

Purpose To explain.

Text structure

(1) Title — Tells the reader what the explanation is about. Often contains how or why.

(2) Introduction — Definition of the subject of the explanation.

(3) Paragraph that describes the parts of the subject or the appearance

(4) Paragraph that explains how or why, usually in time order if explaining a process

(5) Rounding off paragraph — Could include where the subject can be found or what it is used for.

Long tasks

These are long writing tasks, so you have 45 minutes to plan, write and check your writing.

(1) You have come up with a brilliant idea for a new computer game. Write a letter to the game manufacturers explaining how to play and the purpose of the game.

(2) Write an explanation for your ancient great auntie telling her how the TV, DVD, video and home cinema system works, which she has just tried to cook the dinner in!

Short tasks

These are short writing tasks, so you have 20 minutes to plan, write and check your writing.

(1) Write an explanation leaflet that tells the reader how to stop little brothers and sisters from playing with their things.

(2) Write a note to your teacher explaining why you have failed to hand in any of your homework on time since the beginning of the year.

Tip Explanations can be in the form of letters, diagrams, information leaflets, encyclopedia entries and posters.

Non-chronological report

Definition

Non-chronological reports give a reader information about something or somewhere. They are usually about a group of things, e.g. dinosaurs, not one thing in particular, e.g. Dilly the dinosaur. Facts about the subject are organised into paragraphs.

Purpose To give information.

Text structure

1	Title	Usually the subject of the report.
2	Introduction	Definition of the subject of the explanation.
3	Series of paragraphs about various aspects of the subject	
4	Rounding off statement	Could include where the subject can be found or what it is used for.

Long tasks

These are long writing tasks so you have 45 minutes to plan, write and check your writing.

1 Write a report describing the latest craze to hit the playground, "Blademon" the Japanese "battling top" card trading game. What is the game and what effect is it having on schoolchildren across the country?

2 Write a report about the new car you've just built in the Design and Technology lesson for the next James Bond film. Explain all the gadgets and special features.

Short tasks

These are short writing tasks so you have 20 minutes to plan, write and check your writing.

1 Write a short "Guide Book for Parents" for when parents want to visit your classroom.

2 Write a postcard to your best friend telling them all about the luxury 5-star hotel you are staying in on holiday.

Tip Reports can be in the form of letters, encyclopedia entries, information posters or leaflets, as well as straightforward pieces of writing.
A non-chronological report on a school might include headings such as:
● Number of pupils ● After school clubs ● Location
Remember to think about the **purpose** of your writing!

Argument

Definition

An argument gives the reader information about an issue from different points of view, then leaves the reader to make up their mind about how they feel about the issue.

Purpose To present a balanced argument.

Text structure

1. Title — Often in the form of a question.
2. Identify the issue
3. Points to support the issue
4. Points against the issue
5. Summary

Long tasks

These are long writing tasks so you have 45 minutes to plan, write and check your writing.

1. "Children should have a say in how the country is run, so the voting age should be lowered to seven." What are the arguments for and against?

2. "PE lessons should only be attended by pupils who want to take part. Those who want to opt out could do another subject of their choice." Write the arguments for and against this idea.

Short tasks

These are short writing tasks so you have 20 minutes to plan, write and check your writing.

1. List in table form the arguments for and against children using mobile phones in school.

2. List in table form the arguments for and against school canteens selling "fast food" to children at lunchtime.

Tip You might be asked to write an account in the form of a newspaper or magazine article. Remember to back up your ideas with evidence.

Recount

Definition

A recount tells the reader about something that has happened in the past. It might have happened to the writer or to someone else.

Purpose To retell an event or events.

Text structure

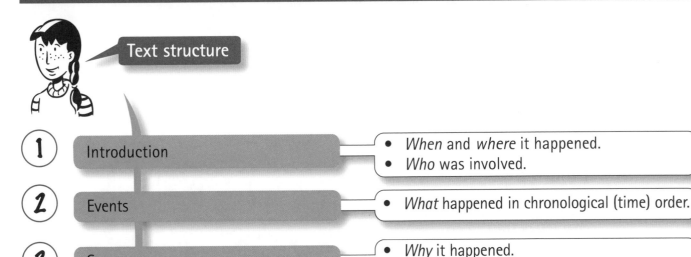

1 Introduction
- *When* and *where* it happened.
- *Who* was involved.

2 Events
- *What* happened in chronological (time) order.

3 Summary
- *Why* it happened.
- *How* someone felt about it.

Long tasks

These are long writing tasks, so you have 45 minutes to plan, write and check your writing.

1 You have just returned to civilisation after a week surviving in the jungle following a plane crash. Write an article for the local newspaper that tells the readers all about your incredible survival against all the odds.

2 The school Sports Day has been a great success and you managed to win all the events you entered. The head teacher has asked you to write an account of the day for the school website. Can you do so without sounding too boastful?

Short tasks

These are short writing tasks, so you have 20 minutes to plan, write and check your writing.

1 Write a diary entry which describes your first day at your new school; "St. Gareth's" – the leading primary for "pop wannabees".

2 You're a reporter for a TV news channel. The editor of the evening news programme has asked you to cover the top story of the day. This morning, it was announced by a top university that a cure had been found for people without any manners. Write some notes for your script for tonight's show, recounting this historic event.

Tip An example of a recount might be a biography, writing about a trip, a newspaper article or an account of an event.

Story structure

All stories are organised in the same basic way.
When you plan and write, think in five sections.

Beginning

Introduce the **main characters** and the **setting**.

Build up

The **story gets going** – the characters start to do something.

Problem

Something goes wrong for the characters. This is the most exciting part.

Resolution

The problem is **sorted** out in some way.

Ending

All the **loose ends are tied up**. The **characters reflect or think** about what happened.

Think of some stories you know or have read recently. Do they fit this pattern?

Story ingredients

Before even planning a story, you need to decide on the three main story ingredients.

Setting

This is WHEN and WHERE the story takes place. You need to help the reader to make a picture in their mind. The setting can also be used to create an atmosphere and affect how the reader feels.

Think about some stories you have read. When and where were they set? How do you know? Look at some short stories to see how the authors have told the reader about the setting. Have a go at drawing the setting that you read about.

Characters

This is WHO is in the story. You need to help the reader build up a picture of the main characters. They need to have an idea of what the characters are like.

Think about some stories you have read. Who were the characters? What were they like? How do you know? What were they called? Look at some short stories to see how authors have told the reader about the characters. Try drawing a character as you see them.

Theme

This is WHAT happens in the story. Some people say that there are only a few story themes in the world. All writers borrow ideas from other stories and this is something you can do.

Think about some stories you have read. What happened? Did one story remind you of any others? List some of the common themes, e.g. good overcoming evil, main character losing something.

Once you've chosen your ingredients, mix them together and make a story!

Settings

Use one of the ideas below to develop a paragraph about a setting. The answer section contains a model answer for the first setting. It is longer than you would be expected to write but will give you ideas for future writing.

1 The fairground didn't feel the same without the music, laughter and flashing lights. The only sound Kelly heard was the faint tapping of loose canvas in the night breeze.

2 The deep snow made each step feel as if she were walking on feather pillows. Normally this would have been fun, but time was running out for her father.

3 The bay opened out before the astonished group as they turned the corner of the rocky headland.

4 The stadium quickly filled with supporters as the kick-off time approached. Ben always felt a tingle of anticipation just before 3 o'clock.

5 The playground seemed like a huge sea of people as Hannah walked through the gates on her first day. Coming to the city was a world away from what she knew before.

Character descriptions

Use one of the ideas below to develop a paragraph about a character. The answer section contains a model answer for the first character. It is longer than you would be expected to write but will give you ideas for future writing.

1 You are the main character in a story, travelling through a hot and dusty country. Describe a small boy you see selling soft drinks and sweets from the side of the road.

2 Introduce the main character in the story who is the guest of honour at a party but is hiding a terrible secret from his/her friends.

3 Describe the character of a retired old soldier who is passing on all his old medals and memories to his great-grandson.

4 Describe a young woman taking her driving test for the fifth time, in her rich father's Rolls Royce.

5 You are a small boy or girl who is the only survivor from a plane crash on a snow-covered mountain. Write a description of the rescuer who pulls you from the wreckage.

Adventure stories

Example James and the Giant Peach

Use the planning sheet below to help you to complete one of the independent writing tasks.

Remember – you should spend about 10 minutes on planning your story, so it's important to practise.

You can draw your own planning sheets using the headings below.

Beginning Introduce the main characters and the setting.	
Build up The story gets going – the characters start to do something.	
Problem Something goes wrong for the characters. This is the most exciting point.	
Resolution The problem is resolved in some way.	
Ending The loose ends are tied up. The characters reflect or think about what happened.	

Independent writing

Plan and write your own adventure story using one of these titles.

1   Escape from Shark Island
2   The Return of the Masked Avenger
3   The Golden Statue and the City of Lost Souls
4   Crisis at 30,000ft!
5   Stranded in the Sahara…
6   Journey to the Bottom of the Sea
7   Rescued!

Myths and legends

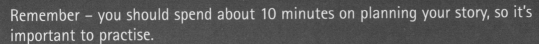

Example King Arthur and his Knights of the Round Table

Use the planning sheet below to help you to complete one of the independent writing tasks.

Remember – you should spend about 10 minutes on planning your story, so it's important to practise.

You can draw your own planning sheets using the headings below.

Beginning Introduce the main characters and the setting.	
Build up The story gets going – the characters start to do something.	
Problem Something goes wrong for the characters. This is the most exciting point.	
Resolution The problem is resolved in some way.	
Ending The loose ends are tied up. The characters reflect or think about what happened.	

Independent writing

Plan and write your own adventure story using one of these titles.

1 Sir Charge and the Dragon
2 How the Tiger Earned His Stripes
3 Why the Grass is Green
4 The Three Tasks of 'Conan the Coward'
5 The Land of the Golden Apples
6 How the Fox Got His Bushy Tail
7 The Legend of 'Noose Snap Jack'

Traditional tales

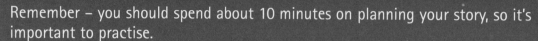

Example Little Red Riding Hood

Use the planning sheet below to help you to complete one of the independent writing tasks.

Remember – you should spend about 10 minutes on planning your story, so it's important to practise.

You can draw your own planning sheets using the headings below.

Beginning Introduce the main characters and the setting.	
Build up The story gets going – the characters start to do something.	
Problem Something goes wrong for the characters. This is the most exciting point.	
Resolution The problem is resolved in some way.	
Ending The loose ends are tied up. The characters reflect or think about what happened.	

Independent writing

Plan and write your own traditional tale using one of these titles.

1   Three Wishes for Princess Glum!
2   The Fairy Godmother Who Lost Her Wand
3   The Three Brothers and the Magic Coin
4   The Wolf and the Shepherd-boy
5   The Magic Cauldron
6   The King Who Lost His Crown
7   The Lady of the Twisting Tower

Modern story

Example The Story of Tracey Beaker

Use the planning sheet below to help you to complete one of the independent writing tasks.

Remember – you should spend about 10 minutes on planning your story, so it's important to practise.

You can draw your own planning sheets using the headings below.

Beginning Introduce the main characters and the setting.	
Build up The story gets going – the characters start to do something.	
Problem Something goes wrong for the characters. This is the most exciting point.	
Resolution The problem is resolved in some way.	
Ending The loose ends are tied up. The characters reflect or think about what happened.	

Independent writing

Plan and write your own modern story using one of these titles.

1   The BMX and Scooter Grand Prix
2   Bad Day at St. Bart's Juniors
3   My Dad Was an Alien!
4   The Strangest Birthday Present
5   How I Got to Be on TV!
6   The Lost Diary
7   The Toy that Came to Life

Science fiction tale

Example The Artemis Fowl series

Use the planning sheet below to help you to complete one of the independent writing tasks.

Remember – you should spend about 10 minutes on planning your story, so it's important to practise.

You can draw your own planning sheets using the headings below.

Beginning Introduce the main characters and the setting.	
Build up The story gets going – the characters start to do something.	
Problem Something goes wrong for the characters. This is the most exciting point.	
Resolution The problem is resolved in some way.	
Ending The loose ends are tied up. The characters reflect or think about what happened.	

Independent writing

Plan and write your own science fiction tale using one of these titles.

1   When Computers Took Over the World!
2   Lost in Deep Space
3   My Best Friend is a Robot
4   Alien Abduction!
5   The Time-Travelling Teacher
6   The Machine that Fixed Everything...
7   Holiday on Mars

Fiction planning grid

Use the planning sheet below to help you to complete one of the independent writing tasks.

Remember – you should spend about 10 minutes on planning your story, so it's important to practise.

You can draw your own planning sheets using the headings below.

Beginning Introduce the main characters and the setting.	
Build up The story gets going – the characters start to do something.	
Problem Something goes wrong for the characters. This is the most exciting point.	
Resolution The problem is resolved in some way.	
Ending The loose ends are tied up. The characters reflect or think about what happened.	

Tip Remember to keep your planning notes short, just the key words to remind you about setting, characters and what is going on.

Reading comprehension

READING BETWEEN THE LINES

When reading a piece of text, you have to look for clues that the writer is giving you. Good writers leave things out and it's up to you to find them.
Look at this example.

> *Freddy ran towards the marquee, his orange trousers flapping wildly, his red wig slipping off his head and his floppy shoes slapping on the pavement. He knew the show had already begun...*

 What colour were Freddy's trousers? The answer to this question is clearly stated in the text.

 What is Freddy dressed as? The text doesn't actually say that Freddy is a clown but from the description of his clothes you can guess with certainty.

 Why do you think Freddy was running? The writer has given you clues. Freddy is running and he knew the show had already begun. This implies he was late for his performance. To say "he was late" isn't good enough here. You must mention that "the show had already begun".

Have a go!

What do you think the author meant if you read between the lines?

"What time is Mummy coming?" the little girl asked anxiously.

"I'm going to get you for that!" Danny Boyle threatened.

Her eyes widened and she slowly raised her hand to her mouth as she surveyed the scene before her.

ENGLISH

Answers for Practice Questions

Answers

Page 8

The passive voice or impersonal writing

1 When playing a match, the eye must not be taken off the ball. Force openings by hitting the ball hard. This will give opponents little time to react.
2 Cars with high fuel consumption are damaging the environment. Fumes from these cars are causing the air quality in cities to fall.
3 When making an omlette, break the eggs into a bowl.

Page 9

Formal descriptions

1 Fast food has health implications for our society. It does not provide a balanced diet. Fresh fruit and vegetables are a healthy alternative.
2 If you have seen a puppy that has been mistreated then you will understand more about the issue of animal cruelty.
3 Using wet clay is an enjoyable but messy activity.
4 Rosie approached the gates of the manor house. She felt something was going to happen. Would the young man be there to meet her?

Page 10

Simple present tense

1 The sunny weather is the main reason people go to Spain for their holidays.
2 Motor racing is a very dangerous sport. Accidents occur often.
3 The Derby is a very famous horse race. It attracts huge crowds of spectators.
4 Gardening is one of the most popular pastimes in this country. Each season gives the gardener something to think about.
5 The train is late because of the dreadful weather we are having today.
6 We are washing up the dirty plates that are lying in the sink.
7 The test is hard but I'm doing my best.

Page 11

Connectives

1 Firstly/first, roll the dice. Secondly/second/next/then/after that, move the counter along the board.
2 The bike went out of control because the tyres were flat. Luckily/however, no one was seriously injured.
3 After the flood, everyone returned to their houses. However/Fortunately, some households were undamaged.
4 After all that's how the Romans became so successful. Anyway what did the Romans ever do for us?
5 Furthermore if you take out our policy we will give you a free cuddly toy. Moreover/also we will give you the first month free.
6 Consequently due to your ridiculous behaviour, we are now banned from playing football at lunchtime. As a result we lost the final.
7 Sometimes/On one hand, people say that skiing is dangerous, however/but/on the other hand, skiers would say that they know the risks.

Page 20
Settings
The fairground didn't feel the same without the music, laughter and flashing lights. The only sound Kelly heard was the faint tapping of loose canvas in the night breeze.

The rides and stalls, all silent and lifeless, appeared like a dinosaur's graveyard in front of her. The necks and heads of creatures long dead stretched into the blue haze and painted prehistoric silhouettes on the dark canvas sky.

Kelly stopped. She sniffed the muggy air and recognised the smell of burnt candy. It seemed to have soaked into every hoarding, rope and plank of wood; in fact some of the stripy poles looked like they could have been cast in sugar.

A sign gently swung above her head. It had become detached from its bindings and the bulbs, which had once made it flash, were lifeless and broken. Kelly could still make out the words in the darkness, 'Children must be accompanied by an adult' in letters which swirled, Victorian style, across the glossy painted board. 'How appropriate!' mocked a man's voice from somewhere very close. Kelly turned her head slowly towards the sound. 'Is that you Dad?' As soon as the words left her mouth, she spun on her heels. Without waiting for a reply Kelly ran blindly into the darkness, her feet barely touching the worn, flattened grass, as the feeling of panic took over.

Page 21
Character descriptions
Hurriedly, I handed over all my change, flipped the ring-pull of the can and gulped the drink as fast as I could. My thirst satisfied, I looked down at the young boy in faded Bermuda shorts who had taken my money. He looked at me cautiously with eyes that held the secrets of someone twice his age. His long bony fingers pocketed the coins in an old satchel without moving his gaze and he remained motionless on his makeshift stool. Rather uncomfortably, I finished my drink, still aware of his stare. I chanced a glance. He was now working his eyes over every part of my body, inspecting each thread of my worn clothes. Then as he seemed to finish, a broad grin stretched across his face and lit up the space between us. He nodded towards the motif on my t-shirt, then lifted one of his fingers, and pointed to his scrawny chest.

'Beckham!!' he yelled as he sprang from his stool and kicked a ball of rags barefoot and with perfect grace

into a nearby collection of dustbins.

Sample answer for Writing Fiction stories (pages 22 to 26)

This story follows the story structure on page 18 and contains elements of a variety of themes. You will be able to identify the setting and the characters fairly easily. Try to find examples of the different themes, such as Lost or found/Wishing or wanting/Good overcoming evil which are shown on pages 22–26.

This story is longer than anything you would be expected to write in your tests.

Try re-writing the story but keep the length down to 5 or 6 paragraphs. The story structure should stay the same – Beginning, Build up, Problem, Resolution, Ending.

Introduction
A long time ago, before the modern world was invented, salt was a very precious thing. That may sound strange, especially when you consider what is important to us today. Long ago, salt was used to preserve food through cold, barren winters. Having enough salt became very important as it ensured that food lasted until the spring. In short, salt saved people's lives. Soon trade in salt became big business. Those people who had too much salt found they were able to sell it to those that didn't have enough. Now, wherever you find big business you will find greedy men, and this is the story of a very greedy man indeed...

How the Sea Became Salty
Beginning
A long time ago in a seaside town there lived an honest fisherman and his wife. Every night he would take his nets and set off in his wooden boat to fish. He would return in the early morning with his catch which his wife would take to the market to sell. By working hard and dealing honestly, the fisherman and his family managed to earn a comfortable living.

Now, not too far away there lived a dishonest fisherman who was jealous of his neighbour and who despised him for his honest nature. However, he kept his wicked thoughts to himself and often asked to accompany the honest fisherman on his night trips to sea. The honest fisherman was a friendly soul who found it hard to see fault in fellow human beings. He never objected to his neighbour's company, even though he found himself doing most of the work.

Build-up

One day, while walking home after a fishing trip, the two fishermen both heard a noise coming from the rocks near the harbour. When they took a closer look, they discovered a beautiful white dolphin had entangled itself in some old fishing nets. The dishonest fisherman wanted to kill the creature with his axe but he was stopped in mid swing by his companion. 'You have enough to eat,' said the honest fisherman as he freed the dolphin. 'If you are hungry, then eat with us tonight.' The dolphin slipped into the waves and was gone in a flash.

Suddenly a strange gnarled little man appeared from nowhere. He had a long white beard full of seaweed and boots made from seashells. He certainly looked very pleased with the fishermen. In fact, he was falling over himself with gratitude. 'Thank you, thank you!' he cried. 'Within that magical dolphin lives the spirit of the sea, and if any harm comes to it then all living things in the sea will slowly die. You must be handsomely rewarded!'

At these words the dishonest fisherman's eyes widened. From out of the air, the little gnarled man produced two small wooden boxes. He laid them carefully on a rock and lifted the lids. Inside the first box was a glistening brooch of shiny gold which sparkled with precious stones. Inside the second box there was a small wooden salt grinder. 'Take your pick,' said the little gnarled man, beaming. Without a thought, the honest fisherman asked his companion which one he would like. Greedily and without a word of thanks, the dishonest fisherman grabbed the brooch and ran off home before somebody changed their mind. It was an offer too good to be true! That left the honest fisherman with the humble salt grinder. But, as you may know from stories such as these, this was no ordinary salt grinder. It was a magic salt grinder and the little gnarled man explained how it worked.

'This salt grinder will grind salt for as long as you wish,' he whispered in a serious tone. 'All you have to say are the words 'Salt grinder, salt grinder, grind my salt. Salt grinder, salt grinder, please don't halt' and you will have an everlasting supply of the wonderful stuff! You will never run out! When you want the grinder to stop grinding salt then you must say these magic words, 'Salt grinder hear my call, please don't grind my salt at all!''

Well, the honest fisherman was delighted with his gift and he thanked the little gnarled man before heading home to his wife, keen to test his magic salt grinder.

When he got home the fisherman told his wife about the unusual events and then with some excitement, placed the salt grinder on their only table. He uttered the words of the little gnarled man.

'Salt grinder, salt grinder, grind my salt. Salt grinder, salt grinder, please don't halt.'

As soon as he spoke the rhyme, a stream of pure white salt poured steadily onto the table forming a neat mountain which soon cascaded onto the floor and gradually started filling the room. The honest fisherman then uttered the second rhyme told to him by the little gnarled man. 'Salt grinder hear my call, please don't grind my salt at all!' and with that the salt grinder stopped the flow of salt. The honest fisherman and his wife looked at each other in astonishment. Without another word they collected all the bags and sacks they had in the cottage and started bagging up all the precious salt that they could. By morning, they had managed to fill the honest fisherman's cart to the brim with the finest salt to sell at market the following day.

Problem

Well, before long the honest fisherman and his wife had made rather a lot of money from selling their salt and soon became very rich and respected in their local area. People would travel from miles around to buy the finest salt that anyone had ever seen. So it wasn't long before the dishonest fisherman heard of their success. He was now a rich merchant himself having sold the wonderful brooch for a small fortune.

Intrigued by his former companion's success, he decided to pay him a call. The dishonest merchant sailed in his beautiful boat to the town where the honest merchant lived. The honest merchant was delighted to see his old neighbour and before long they were talking about how their lives had changed since the day they they had chanced upon the magic dolphin. The dishonest merchant was desperate to find out about the salt grinder and begged the honest merchant to show him how he was able to produce so much fine quality salt. The honest merchant had kept his salt grinder a secret from everyone else and was reluctant to show anyone how it worked. No matter how hard he tried, the dishonest merchant could not get the honest merchant to share his secret. Seething with jealousy, the dishonest merchant made his excuses and left, only to return secretly that night under the cover of darkness.

This time he was determined to find out about the magic salt grinder, and if it could make him even richer. He peered in through a window of the house just in time to see the honest merchant's wife place the grinder on the table and say the magic words, 'Salt grinder, salt grinder, grind my salt. Salt grinder, salt grinder, please don't halt.' The dishonest merchant watched in amazement as the grinder produced a gushing flow of precious salt which the honest merchant's wife channelled into sacks. The dishonest merchant ducked down from the window in disbelief. He simply had to own that grinder! With it he would become the richest man in the world. He popped his head up to the window again and saw a golden opportunity. The grinder was sitting on the table, it had stopped flowing with salt and the honest merchant's wife had left the room. Without thinking twice, the dishonest merchant slipped in and out of the window in a trice and ran off carrying the precious grinder.

Resolution
He didn't look back. He set sail into the night, delighted with his daring exploits and laughing with excitement at the thought of the riches he knew would be his. Halfway into his voyage home, he could contain himself no longer. The urge to start making his fortune even greater was too much. The dishonest merchant took out the salt grinder and placed it on the deck of his boat. He chanted the magic words that he had heard the honest merchant's wife recite that evening. 'Salt grinder, salt grinder, salt grinder, grind my salt. Salt grinder, salt grinder, please don't halt.' The grinder burst into life seemingly producing salt faster than ever. Within minutes the boat was full of mounds of salt and the dishonest merchant was frantically screaming for the grinder to stop. The greedy man didn't know the magic words. The grinder churned out the salt so quickly that the boat became heavier and heavier and soon the sea water started to flow over the sides. Within seconds the boat began to sink and the dishonest merchant and the magic salt grinder disappeared beneath the waves.

Ending
The honest merchant and his wife never found out what had happened to their gift. They were good people and were happy with the money and friends they had made and lived contentedly without it. The magic salt grinder, of course, still lies at the bottom of the sea to this day. It still makes salt and will continue to do so until it hears the magic words. And you can be sure, that won't be for a long, long time to come.

Page 31
Treasure Island
1 Jim started writing his account in 1700.
2 The old sailor's coat was blue.
3 The scar on the sailor's cheek was caused by a sabre cut.
4 The sailor asked for a glass of rum.
5 The sailor said they could call him 'Captain'.
6 'Nut-brown' implies that the sailor had a deep sun-tan which sailors would have had in those days because most of their time would have been spent outdoors on deck.
7 The phrase that tells us why Jim can't give the island's position away is 'because there is still treasure not yet lifted'. This implies that lots of treasure was taken off the island and they want to go back to collect the rest.
8 The sailor is described as being tall, strong, heavy, nut-brown, having ragged and scarred hands, having a sabre scar across his cheek, having black, broken nails and wearing a soiled coat. The reader is also aware that he has a liking for rum and for singing old sea-songs. All this evidence points to life at sea being very tough in the 18th century.
9 Both yes or no are valid answers but both must be backed up by three reasons which refer to the text that have caused you to think that way.
10 Three points which are related to the text should be included in the diary entry. These might include, amongst others, the fact that business was not good so they were grateful for the custom; the new guest looked very suspicious with his sabre scars; the new guest, despite his appearance, was able to pay in advance with gold coins; or maybe they had better get fresh supplies of bacon, eggs and rum as the sailor had made his preferences clear and intended to stay a long time.

Page 33
Charm School
1 The third floor.
2 He put his foot in the doors.
3 Dolls.
4 Miss Cute Candy.
5 Diamanté.
The following answers could vary.
6 He thought she needed to learn charm when she made a face at him.
7 She is dreading going into the charm school even more now she has seen the pictures that look like dolls.
8 It doesn't say anything on the Woodwork 1 sheet about needing sticking plasters.
   Or on the Practical Parenting sheet about bringing your aspirins.
9 The author uses adverbs to describe how Bonny says things. Stubbornly, coolly, nervously.
10 Answers will vary.

Page 35

The Magic Box

1 Any 3 of the following: blue, violet, black, white, yellow.
2 Last – the joke of an ancient uncle. First – the smile of a baby.
3 The swish of a silk sari on a summer night.
   The tip of a tongue touching a tooth.
4 Secrets.
5 Surf.
6 The snowman is hungry.
7 Made out of.
8 Answers could vary. Reverses the usual image which makes you look differently at usual images.
9 Answers will vary.
10 Answers will vary.

Pages 38-39

Shark Attack

1 The average number of unprovoked attacks is 75.
2 Because shiny jewellery resembles fish scales.
3 Because divers have been grabbing or feeding sharks while underwater.
4 25 million sharks are killed by humans each year.
5 The Basking Shark lives off the shores of Great Britain and receives government protection.
6 The hit-and-run attack is least likely to result in death because the shark makes one attack, injuries are
   minor and the shark leaves the area. (One of these reasons for a mark.)
7 No, it's not a good idea to fish for sharks because you run the risk of an unprovoked attack and there are
   already 25 million sharks killed by fishing each year. (There is no evidence in the text to suggest that
   fishing for sharks is a good idea, so a 'yes' answer = 0 marks.)
8 Fact, opinion, fact, fact, fact, opinion, fact.
9 Three points of advice needed for three marks. One of these must be 'not to grab or feed any sharks' and
   any two other relevant points from the text.
10 A yes or no answer will do as long as the opinion is supported by references to the text. For example: I did
   enjoy reading this article because I found out some unusual facts about sharks. I was amazed that only 10
   deaths occur on average each year through shark attacks. There were some very useful tips such as
   'always swim in a group' and 'don't wander too far from shore'. These would apply any time you swam in
   the sea.

Page 43

Spelling puzzle

You should spell out the message: Level four is a doddle!

Page 44

Capital letters and full stops

1 The intense July heat made Pat feel quite dizzy.
2 It wasn't what Alex had wanted but who cared about that?
3 What shall I do in Rome this weekend?
4 It often rains on Monday mornings.
5 Leo remembered that he had seen her the previous Saturday.
6 December means Christmas.
7 H.G. Wells once lived in Bromley in Kent.
8 Michael loved great artists such as Pablo Picasso.

Page 45

Commas

The early movies gave us comedy greats like Laurel and Hardy, Buster Keaton, Harold Lloyd and Charlie
Chaplin.
Audiences loved their comic timing, wit, invention and grace.
In their films they used everyday items as props like hats, ties, glasses and walking sticks.
City Lights, The Great Dictator, The Kid and The Gold Rush are four of Charlie Chaplin's best films.

Page 46

Direct Speech

"What a wonderful day for taking a boat out on the lake," said Ollie joyfully.

"Sure is," Stan answered, "but how about a cool drink beforehand?"

"Great idea," replied Ollie, "except we've only got three pound coins. We've got to buy the girls one as well."

"What can we do?" replied Stan.

"I know," schemed Ollie. "When I ask you what you'd like to drink, you refuse."

"But!"

"No buts," hurried Ollie. "Here are the girls. Now then, a cola for you, a cola for you and a cola for me. Stanley, what will you have?"

"A cola."

"Can't you grasp the situation? We've only got three pounds. When I ask you what you want you must refuse."

"Oh," beamed Stan.

"Sorry girls," grinned Ollie as he regained his composure. "So that's a cola, a cola, a cola and my dear Stanley, what will you have."

"A cola."

"Why do you keep saying a cola?" pleaded Ollie.

"Because you keep asking me," cried Stan.

Page 47

Apostrophes

The boys' books were in a terrible state.

Sofie's marks were excellent when she studied.

Philip's shoes were never clean.

I wouldn't be visiting that shop again.

Katie didn't finish her work on time.

Elizabeth's homework got great marks.

I hadn't got my pocket money yet.

Tim's class wasn't over until the evening.

The girls' dance routine shouldn't take more than 5 minutes.

John's feet didn't touch the ground.

Page 48-49

There was a candle burning on a table in the hall, and a smell of onions, gravy and roast beef.

"Anybody home?" called Jackson, up a grand staircase that lost itself in shadows.

"Home" came down an echo "Home – home – home!"

"I brung back your dog!"

"Dog – dog – dog!"

"I've got to be going now!"

"Now – now – now!"

"Well," said Jackson. "Somebody must be about. Somebody must have lit the candle. Maybe they've fallen asleep."

He began to look first in one room, then in another, then in another. They were all dark and nobody answered when he called. He went upstairs, and the dog followed after, growling and whining all the way. There was a glimmer of light coming from under a door. Jackson knocked. No answer. He called. No answer. He turned the handle and went inside.

Pages 50-51

Answers will vary.

Page 52

Nouns and verbs
Answers will vary.

Adjectives
Suggested adjectives.

Funny, bright, carefree	Black, dark, evil
Tiny, faithful, loyal	Ferocious, enormous, terrifying
Squeaky, happy, infectious	Evil, deep, grating
Sweet, soft, happy	Booming, fierce, barking

Page 53

Adverbs
Answers will vary.

Alliteration
Suggested answers.
He sighed slowly before he spoke.
The bowl was perfectly placed to show off the flowers.
When she saw the mess, she briskly brushed it all away.
They all laughed loudly at the end of the performance.

ABOUT THE READING TEST

In the test, you should read the questions very carefully so that you fully understand what you are being asked. You will be expected to:

- make sense of what you are reading

- find information and ideas in a text

- work out what the author meant

- work out why a text is organised in a particular way

- say something about the vocabulary and style that an author has used

- say something about how a text makes you feel

- link what you read to your own life

★ Tips

- In your reading test, the questions ask for 1, 2 or 3 mark answers.

- If an answer is worth 1 mark you can find the answer on the page. You are being asked to find a particular word, phrase or piece of information. These questions are obviously the easiest but you still need to read and answer them carefully.

- If an answer is worth 2 or 3 marks, you are being asked to work out what the author meant. These questions are obviously harder but you get more marks!

- Always support your 2 and 3 mark answers with evidence and examples from the text.

- If you get a question that starts "What do you think ..." or "How do you know ..." you are being asked for your opinion. Always use examples from the text to back up your answer.

Treasure Island

These questions are about the opening paragraphs to the classic adventure story *Treasure Island* by Robert Louis Stevenson.

The story was written over 100 years ago but it still remains popular today and has recently been adapted for the film *Treasure Planet*.

Some of the language needs to be read quite carefully and it helps if you can picture the scene.

The person talking at the beginning of the story is the hero of the tale – a boy called Jim Hawkins. He is remembering how his adventures began when a mysterious character turned up at his parents' inn, 'The Admiral Benbow', looking for a place to stay.

Part One – The Old Buccaneer

Chapter 1: The Old Sea-dog at the Admiral Benbow

Squire Trelawney, Dr. Livesey, and the rest of these gentlemen having asked me to write down the whole particulars about Treasure Island, from the beginning to the end, keeping nothing back but the bearings of the island, and that only because there is still treasure not yet lifted, I take up my pen in the year of grace 1700 and go back to the time when my father kept the Admiral Benbow inn and the brown old seaman with the sabre cut first took up his lodging under our roof.

I remember him as if it were yesterday, as he came plodding to the inn door, his sea-chest following behind him in a hand-barrow – a tall, strong, heavy, nut-brown man, his tarry pigtail falling over the shoulder of his soiled blue coat, his hands ragged and scarred, with black, broken nails, and the sabre cut across one cheek, a dirty, livid white. I remember him looking round the cove and whistling to himself as he did so, and then breaking out in that old sea-song that he sang so often afterwards:

"Fifteen men on the dead man's chest –

Yo-ho-ho, and a bottle of rum!"

in the high, old tottering voice that seemed to have been tuned and broken at the capstan bars. Then he rapped on the door with a bit of stick like a handspike that he carried, and when my father appeared, called roughly for a glass of rum. This, when it was brought to him, he drank slowly, like a connoisseur, lingering on the taste and still looking about him at the cliffs and up at our signboard.

"This is a handy cove," says he at length; "and a pleasant sittyated grog-shop. Much company, mate?"

My father told him no, very little company, the more was the pity.

"Well, then," said he, "this is the berth for me. Here you, matey," he cried to the man who trundled the barrow; "bring up alongside and help up my chest. I'll stay here a bit," he continued. "I'm a plain man; rum and bacon and eggs is what I want, and that head up there for to watch ships off. What you mought call me? You mought call me captain. Oh, I see what you're at – there"; and he threw down three or four gold pieces on the threshold. "You can tell me when I've worked through that," says he, looking as fierce as a commander.

These questions are worth one mark each.

1 In which year did Jim start writing his account of his adventures?

1 mark

2 What colour was the old sailor's coat?

1 mark

3 What caused the cut across the sailor's cheek?

1 mark

4 What was the first thing the sailor asked for when Jim's father answered the door?

1 mark

5 By what name did the sailor wish to be known?

1 mark

These questions are worth two marks each. If you need more space use extra paper.

6 The visitor is described as "the brown old seaman" and a "nut-brown man". Why would this be a fitting description for someone who worked onboard a ship?

2 marks

7 Jim has been asked to "write down the whole particulars about Treasure Island" but not to tell where the island actually is. Can you find a phrase in the text which tells us why he can't let us know?

2 marks

8 What does the description of the sailor tell you about life at sea in the 18th century? Give reasons for your answer.

2 marks

These questions are worth three marks each. If you need more space use extra paper.

9 Does this opening to the story make you want to read on? Give reasons for your opinion.

3 marks

10 Imagine you are Jim's father, the landlord of "The Admiral Benbow". What would you write in your diary for that day?

3 marks

Total marks

Charm School

Bonny got out of the lift on the third floor, as she'd been told, and stamped her foot.

"Horrible!" she muttered. "Horrible, horrible, horrible! I hate this town. I hate this place. I hate the world. I hate everybody!"

"Wrong floor, I think," a voice beside her said.

Bonny spun round and told the man hurrying round the corner into the lift, "This is three, isn't it? Where I'm supposed to be?"

He looked her up and down. "I don't think so, Little Miss Grumpy. Unless, of course, you're here to help Maura with the sound and the lighting. The only people on this floor today are Mrs Opalene's pupils."

"That's right," Bonny said stubbornly. "And I'm one of them."

"Oh, yes?" As if to show how little he believed her, he put his foot in the lift doorway to stop it closing. "So where's all your stuff?"

A tinned voice spurted out of the lift ceiling. "*Please check the doors for obstructions.*"

Startled, the man drew back his foot. The lift doors closed.

Fed up with people as good as telling her to her face that she was a Charm-free Zone, Bonny seized the opportunity to stick out her tongue, dig her thumbs in her ears, and waggle her fingers.

The lift doors opened again and the man stared.

"I was quite wrong," he said before they closed again properly. "You were quite right. This is quite obviously the floor you need."

All along the corridor were photographs of dolls. All sorts of dolls, from innocent blue-eyed china dolls to mischievous dark-eyed dolls. But all had shiny eyes with curly lashes, and clouds of perfect hair, and pearly teeth behind their painted, triumphant smiles. They all had names as well, printed beneath the pictures. Miss Rosebud, one was called. Miss Sweet Caroline was another. Little Miss Cute Candy hung between Princess Royale and Our Million Dollar Baby. And Miss Stardust even had a wand to match her glittery frock.

Along the corridor came the tea boy, pushing his trolley. "Are you lost?" he asked Bonny.

"No. I just stopped to look."

"Choosing your favourite?"

Bonny stared at him coolly. "I don't think so. I'm a bit old for dollies."

The tea boy nodded at the pictures. "Never too old to look like a twink."

Bonny took a closer look at Miss Cute Candy. "Are you *serious*? Are you telling me she's *real*?"

"*Real*?" said the tea boy. "She's a tiger, that one. She just this minute bit my head off for running a trolley wheel over one of her diamanté shoes."

"What's diamanté?"

"Don't ask me," he shrugged. "That's what she called it when she threw her little tantrum."

"Where is she now?" asked Bonny, a little nervously.

"Where do you think?" said the tea boy. "She's behind that door with the others, spending the day in Charm School."

Bonny was horrified. "It didn't say!" she wailed. "It didn't say anything on the pink sheet about dressing up like dollies!"

The tea boy shrugged. "So? It doesn't say anything on the Woodwork I sheet about needing sticking plasters. Or on the Practical Parenting sheet about bringing your aspirins."

"It's going to be *awful*, isn't it?" Bonny said.

From *Charm School* by Anne Fine

These questions are worth one mark each.

1 On which floor was Bonny told to leave the lift?

1 mark — 1

2 How did the man in the lift stop the doors from closing?

1 mark — 2

3 At first, what did Bonny think the photographs were?

1 mark — 3

4 Who did the tea boy describe as "a tiger"?

1 mark — 4

5 How did Little Miss Cute Candy describe her shoes?

1 mark — 5

These questions are worth two marks each. If you need more space use extra paper.

6 Why did the man in the lift tell Bonny he was wrong?

2 marks — 6

7 '"It didn't say!" she wailed.' What does the author want you to think about Bonnie at this point in the story?

2 marks — 7

8 Find two examples of something the tea boy says that show he has a sense of humour.

2 marks — 8

These questions are worth three marks each. If you need more space use extra paper.

9 How has the author built up the reader's understanding of Bonny's personality? Write three examples from the extract to support your opinion.

3 marks — 9

10 How do you think Bonny is going to feel when she opens the door to Charm School?

3 marks — 10

Total marks

The Magic Box

By Kit Wright

I will put in the box

the swish of a silk sari on a summer night,
fire from the nostrils of a Chinese dragon,
the tip of a tongue touching a tooth.

I will put in the box

a snowman with a rumbling belly
a sip of the bluest water from Lake Lucerne,
a leaping spark from an electric fish.

I will put into the box

three violet wishes spoken in Gujarati,
the last joke of an ancient uncle,
and the first smile of a baby.

I will put into the box

a fifth season and a black sun,
a cowboy on a broomstick
and a witch on a white horse.

My box is fashioned from ice and gold and steel,
with stars on the lid and secrets in the corners.
Its hinges are the toe joints of dinosaurs.

I shall surf in my box
on the great high-rolling breakers of the wild Atlantic,
then wash ashore on a yellow beach
the colour of the sun.

These questions are worth one mark each.

1 Write down three colour words the poet has used as adjectives.

1 mark
1

2 What two things does the poet describe as "last" and "first"?

2
1 mark

3 Write down two lines from the poem where the poet has used alliteration.

3
1 mark

4 What does the magic box have in its corners?

4
1 mark

5 What does the poet intend to do with the magic box?

5
1 mark

These questions are worth two marks each. If you need more space use extra paper.

6 The poet says the snowman has a rumbling belly. What does this tell you about the snowman?

6
2 marks

7 What does the poet mean when he says "My box is fashioned..."?

7
2 marks

8 In the stanza beginning "a fifth season", what does the poet do to the images of the cowboy and witch, and what effect does this have?

8
2 marks

These questions are worth three marks each. If you need more space use extra paper.

9 Write a sentence to describe your opinion about the images of "a fifth season" and "a black sun".

9
3 marks

10 What effect do you think the poet wants the last two lines to have on readers?

10
3 marks

Total marks

Shark Attack

Read the information below about sharks and try to answer the questions that follow on pages 38 to 39.

How to Avoid a Shark Attack!

The chances of being attacked by a shark are very small. The yearly average of unprovoked shark attacks on humans is 75, resulting in about 10 deaths. These numbers are tiny if you think about the millions of people who enter the water each year. You have more chance of being struck by lightning than suffering a shark attack. However, to decrease your already small chance of becoming a victim, if you do enter the seas and oceans, then always follow these rules:

1. **Always swim in a group.** Sharks most often attack lone individuals.

2. **Don't wander too far from shore.** Doing so isolates you and places you away from assistance.

3. **Don't enter the water if you're bleeding.** Sharks can smell and taste blood and trace it back to where it came from.

4. **Avoid the water at night, dawn or dusk.** Many sharks are most active at these times and are better equipped to find you than you are to see them.

5. **Don't wear shiny jewellery.** The reflected light looks like shining fish scales.

6. **Don't splash a lot.** Erratic movements can look like an animal in distress and can attract sharks.

7. **If attacked by a shark, the general rule is:** 'Do whatever it takes to get away!'

Types of Shark Attack

➤ **Provoked attacks** are caused by humans touching sharks. Often this involves unhooking sharks or removing them from fishing nets. However, recently there have been a number of incidents involving divers who were attacked after grabbing or feeding a shark while underwater.

➤ **Unprovoked attacks** happen when sharks make the first contact. This can take three forms:

● **Hit-and-run attacks** happen near beaches. In pounding surf, strong currents and murky waters, the movements of humans can often be mistaken for the shark's normal food – fish. The shark will take one bite, let go and immediately leave the area. Legs or feet are often bitten; injuries are usually minor and deaths rarely occur.

● **Sneak attacks** take place in deeper waters. The victim doesn't see the shark coming and the result can be serious injury or death, especially if the shark continues to attack.

● **Bump-and-bite attacks** happen when the shark circles and actually bumps the victim with its head or body before biting. As in the sneak attack, the shark may attack repeatedly and cause serious injury or death.

Sharks Under Attack

Although sharks rarely kill humans, humans are killing about 25 million sharks each year through sport and commercial fishing. Despite being one of the most successful predators ever, they are easily caught themselves by a baited hook or well-placed net. In many areas of the world, sharks are becoming seriously threatened and certain species, such as the Great White, Sand Tiger and Great Britain's native Basking Shark, have received special government protection. From this sort of evidence it is clear that sharks have far more to fear from humans than we do from sharks. Something to think about if you ever take an early evening swim in tropical waters...!

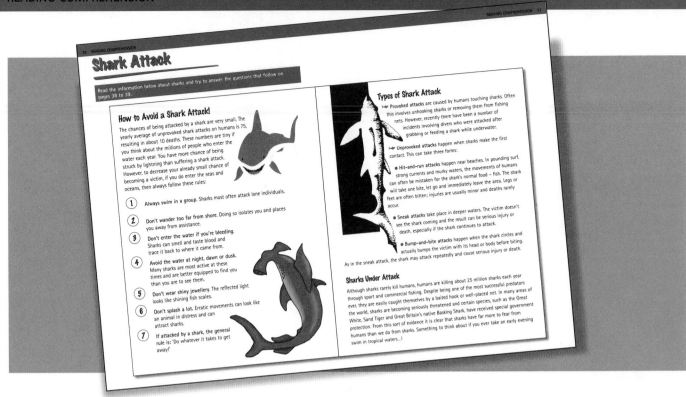

These questions are worth one mark each.

1 What is the average number of unprovoked shark attacks each year?

1 mark · 1

2 Why shouldn't you wear shiny jewellery when swimming?

1 mark · 2

3 Why have there been a number of divers attacked recently?

1 mark · 3

4 How many sharks are killed by humans each year?

1 mark · 4

5 Which shark lives off the shores of Great Britain and receives special government protection?

1 mark · 5

These questions are worth two marks each. If you need more space use extra paper.

6 Which type of shark attack is least likely to result in death and why?

2 marks · 6

7 Do you think it's a good idea to fish for sharks? Give reasons for your answer and refer to the text.

2 marks · 7

8 Fill in this table by placing a tick in either the 'fact' or 'opinion' boxes.
(1–3 correct = 0 marks, 4–5 correct = 1 mark, 6–7 correct = 2 marks)

	Fact	Opinion
Sharks are successful predators		
This article is interesting		
More sharks are killed by humans than humans killed by sharks		
Your chances of being attacked by a shark are very small indeed		
The Great White has received government protection		
Sharks are very frightening		
Sharks are easily caught in nets and on lines		

8

2 marks

These questions are worth three marks each. If you need more space use extra paper.

9 Using the information in the article, what advice would you give a diver about avoiding a shark attack?

_____

_____

_____

_____

9

3 marks

10 Did you enjoy reading this article? Give reasons for your answer.

_____

_____

_____

_____

10

3 marks

Total marks

Spelling rules

Over the next four pages there are a number of spelling lists, spelling rules and spelling games. You will already know some words but you may be unsure of the meaning of others. It would be really useful to learn how to spell all of these words and with time spent learning them – a little and often is best – there is no reason why you can't.

Look, Say, Cover, Write and Check

The tried and tested method of 'Look, Say, Cover, Write and Check' works very well for most people, so give it a go.

Look at the word on the page.

Say the word in your head or out loud.

Cover the word with your hand.

Write the word.

Check the word by lifting your hand.

Mnemonics

Another way to remember spellings is by using mnemonics. A mnemonic is a silly way of remembering something. Take the word 'C O U G H'. Each letter can stand for a new word in an easy to remember phrase.

Colds	C
Open	O
Up	U
Green	G
Hankies!	H

This is a useful way of remembering how to spell tricky words or those words that, for some reason, you keep getting wrong.

Learning to spell new words is not much use on its own. When you can spell a new word correctly, make sure you are aware of what it means and try to use it in your writing. This will give your written work more power and, at the same time, widen your vocabulary, so you can express yourself more freely.

Spelling lists

List 1

Here is a list of the 100 most common words. You probably know most or all of them already. Don't go any further until you can spell each one correctly!

the	Mum	with	a	much	people	been	him	are	but
as	Dad	your	on	to	in	how	through	have	many
not	draw	write	they	this	by	good	it	when	do
may	can	colour	I	we	his	place	from	their	only
each	there	tree	should	other	some	that	an	use	any
up	two	has	dog	what	than	he	had	out	make
no	such	about	cat	its	would	if	them	could	be
because	must	then	climb	first	very	were	made	new	one
of	see	water	time	went	more	into	same	you	these
or	and	like	also	over	under	number	work	which	so

List 2

Here is another list of keywords. You should have learnt these by the end of Year 4. Now's the chance to see if you did. Don't go any further until you have!

above	change	gone	morning	round	though	used
across	coming	heard	near	second	thought	walk
almost	didn't	high	never	show	today	watch
before	different	inside	often	sometimes	together	while
began	does	jumped	only	started	told	without
being	every	knew	other	still	tries	woke
below	following	know	outside	stopped	under	write
better	found	leave	place	such	until	year
between	goes	might	right	think	upon	young

List 3

Here is a list of words that don't spell the way they sound. Most don't follow any of the regular spelling rules so often catch out many people. Learn them all. If you get stuck on one or two then think of a mnemonic to help you remember.

beautiful	nation	weight	
business	special	February	
scream	whistle	library	
dream	listen	address	
height	which	autumn	
minute	lacy	except	
aeroplane	scary	jewellery	
encyclopedia	laugh	write	
machine	thought	wreck	

List your mnemonics here:

Spelling puzzle

Here is a spelling puzzle for you to solve. If you answer the questions correctly then a message will be spelt out for you down the side of the page.

- If the first is wrong, colour in the box under '1st'.

- If the second is wrong, colour in the box under '2nd' and so on.

- Only leave the box that matches the correct spelling.

- When all your answers are correct, a message will be left down the side of the grid.

	First	Second	Third	Fourth	1st	2nd	3rd	4th
1	cabage	cabbage	cabbige	cabidge	A	L	T	N
2	nauty	nawty	naughty	nawghty	C	P	E	E
3	knuckle	nuckle	knukle	knuckal	V	O	S	R
4	lisen	listin	lissen	listen	B	F	G	E
5	messure	measure	mezure	meazer	T	L	N	I
6	believable	believeable	believible	beleevable	F	S	Q	W
7	obeedient	obedient	obediant	obbedient	A	O	B	M
8	whistel	whissel	wistle	whistle	I	D	E	U
9	luxureous	luxurious	luxuryous	lucksurious	S	R	H	Z
10	immitate	imitate	immetate	imeetate	I	I	R	P
11	anoyance	annoyance	annoyence	anoyanse	S	S	B	E
12	excep	except	exseot	eksept	F	A	H	G
13	razer	rauzir	razeor	razor	J	L	K	D
14	laughter	lafter	laffter	laughtor	O	T	A	O
15	answird	answerd	answered	ansered	N	T	D	Y
16	emteed	emptied	empteed	emptid	Y	D	Q	R
17	conseeted	concieted	conceeted	conceited	M	O	C	L
18	pyrramid	pirramid	pyramid	piramyd	J	R	E	N

The message reads ... _____

Punctuation

Punctuation allows you to mark your writing so that the reader knows how to read it.

Capital letters and full stops

- Every sentence should start with a capital letter and end with a full stop (.), question mark (?) or exclamation mark (!).
- Names of people, places, days of the week and months of the year all start with a capital letter. Make sure that your capitals are clear and look different from your lower case letters. Write out the alphabet in capitals, then in lower case, to check that they are clearly different.

Can you re-write these sentences using the correct punctuation?

1 the intense july heat made pat feel quite dizzy

2 it wasn't what alex had wanted but who cared about that

3 what shall I do in rome this weekend

4 it often rains on monday mornings

5 leo remembered that he had seen her the previous saturday

6 december means christmas

7 h g wells once lived in bromley in kent

8 michael loved great artists such as pablo picasso

Commas

A comma is a punctuation mark that separates a part of a sentence. Commas are used:

* to separate names, adjectives or items in a list –
  They took crisps, sandwiches and a bottle of lemonade to the park.
  OR
  Bobby, George, Dennis and Alex were all members of the winning team.
  Notice that you don't need a comma before the last item in the list. Use 'and' instead.
* to give extra information – *Mr Cooper, my teacher, is leaving next week.*
* after a subordinate clause – *In spite of the number of guards, he still managed to escape.*

Try saying a sentence out loud before you write it down. It will help you to 'hear' where the commas should go.

Re-write these sentences adding in the commas.

1 The early movies gave us comedy greats like Laurel and Hardy Buster Keaton Harold Lloyd and Charlie Chaplin.

2 Audiences loved their comic timing wit invention and grace.

3 In their films they used everyday items as props like hats ties glasses and walking sticks.

4 City Lights The Great Dictator The Kid and The Gold Rush are four of Charlie Chaplin's best films.

Speech punctuation

Direct speech

Direct Speech punctuation allows you to use the speaker's actual words inside speech marks (" "). You also need to insert a comma at the end of the speech but INSIDE the last speech mark.

If you start the sentence with the speaker and the speech verb then the comma goes BEFORE the first speech mark. The speech then starts with a capital letter.

If the speaker and the speech verb are in the middle of the speech, then the second section of speech does NOT start with a capital letter because it's all one sentence. In this case a comma goes INSIDE the last speech mark, before the speaker and speech verb, and another comma goes AFTER the speech verb!

Practice question

Use what you have learned about direct speech punctuation to punctuate this conversation. It is based on a script from a Laurel and Hardy film called *Men O' War* made in 1929. Stan and Ollie are two sailors on shore leave. They have just met two girls in the park and they're keen to make a good impression...

Re-write the speech, putting in the missing **speech marks** to bring the situation to life!

What a wonderful day for taking a boat out on the lake, said Ollie joyfully.

Sure is, Stan answered but how about a cool drink beforehand.

Great idea, replied Ollie except we've only got three pound coins. We've got to buy the girls one as well.

What can we do? replied Stan.

I know, schemed Ollie. When I ask you what you'd like to drink, you refuse.

But!

No buts, hurried Ollie. Here are the girls. Now then, a cola for you, a cola for you and a cola for me. Stanley, what will you have?

A cola.

Can't you grasp the situation? We've only got three pound coins. When I ask you what you want you must refuse.

Oh, beamed Stan.

Sorry girls, grinned Ollie as he regained his composure. So that's a cola, a cola, a cola and my dear Stanley, what will you have?

A cola.

Why do you keep saying a cola? pleaded Ollie.

Because you keep asking me, cried Stan.

Apostrophes

Apostrophes to show possession

We use apostrophes to show that something belongs to somebody (possession).
The cat's pyjamas!
Remember – if the noun is plural the apostrophe moves.
The cats' pyjamas!

Apostrophes to show omission

We also use apostrophes to show that a letter has been missed out (omission).
Did not becomes *didn't.*

Practice questions

Re-write these sentences adding in the apostrophes where they are needed. Watch out for the last three!

The boys books were in a terrible state. (plural)

Sofies marks were excellent when she studied.

Philips shoes were never clean.

I would not be visiting that shop again.

Katie did not finish her work on time.

Elizabeths homework got great marks.

I had not got my pocket money yet.

Tims class was not over until the evening.

The girls dance routine should not take more than five minutes. (plural)

Johns feet did not touch the ground.

Test your punctuation

This passage has had all the punctuation taken out. Your challenge is to re-write the passage on the page opposite putting in the correct punctuation. The number of capital letters, full stops, commas, question marks, exclamation marks, apostrophes and sets of speech marks is given beneath the passage. Can you find the correct home for them all?

Read through it before you start and try to 'hear' it in your head. Remember, punctuation gives a 'voice' to your writing.

there was a candle burning on a table in the hall and a smell of onions gravy and roast beef

anybody home called jackson up a grand staircase that lost itself in shadows

home came down an echo home – home – home

I brung back your dog

dog – dog – dog

I ve got to be going now

now – now – now

well said jackson somebody must be about

somebody must have lit the candle maybe theyve fallen asleep

he began to look first in one room then in another then in another they were all dark and nobody answered when he called he went upstairs and the dog followed after growling and whining all the way there was a glimmer of light coming from under a door jackson knocked no answer he called no answer he turned the handle and went inside

Punctuation marks missing	How many to include
Capital letters	23
Full stops	15
Commas	8
Question marks	1
Exclamation marks	5
Apostrophes	2
Sets of speech marks	9

Mind your language

Choose your words carefully... Knowing how to spell lots of words is not much use unless you know how to use them. 'Variety' is the spice of life – and a varied vocabulary improves your writing!

Simile

A simile is where a writer has compared the subject to something else. Usually the writer will use *like* or *as*, e.g. *As brave as a lion or he runs like the wind.*

Invent similes for the following.

1. Peace	6. A diamond
2. Anger	7. A smell
3. A sports car	8. Laughing
4. Falling	9. A bowl of custard
5. Someone's face	10. A new born baby

Metaphor

A metaphor is when the writer writes about something as if it really was something else, e.g. *He is dynamite. Every goal he scores is explosive!*

Write your own sentences containing these metaphors.

1   the clouds raced

_____
_____

2   a river of tears

_____
_____

3   a spring morning smile

_____
_____

4 light ready to leap

_____

_____

5 the snow was a coat

_____

_____

6 huge elephant steps

_____

_____

Personification

Personification is a type of metaphor. It is when the writer gives non-human objects or ideas human characteristics.

Example

The drain gurgled with satisfaction as the keys disappeared through the grate.

Describe these nouns using personification.

1. The storm	4. The pram
2. The oak tree	5. The castle
3. The steam train	6. The picture

Nouns and verbs

Choosing accurate nouns and powerful verbs can sometimes improve your writing more than just adding adjectives and adverbs.

Make these sentences more interesting by choosing better nouns and verbs.

1 The girl looked quickly around the room and smiled.

_____

_____

2 The time went by slowly but at last the car came down the road.

_____

_____

3 The little baby birds in the nesting box were looking out of the hole as if they wanted to leave.

_____

_____

4 "Whose shoe is that?" asked the teacher angrily.

_____

_____

Adjectives

Use adjectives to help your reader get a clear picture of what you mean, e.g. _an ugly crowd_ is very different from _a jubilant crowd_.

Add an adjective to the words in the first column to create a happy mood and in the second column to create a different mood.

_____	look	_____	look
_____	dog	_____	dog
_____	laugh	_____	laugh
_____	voice	_____	voice

Adverbs

An adverb can clarify the meaning of a verb. Sometimes adverbs can be phrases, e.g. *ran like the wind.*
Do not use adverbs that mean the same as the verb, e.g. *whispered quietly.*

Write two sentences using each verb but a different adverb in a sentence. Notice how the meaning changes.

listened	
tapped	
kicked	
slept	
hummed	

Alliteration

Using words with the same initial sound can improve your writing, e.g. *He wearily watched as they left.*

Add an alliterative adverb to these sentences.

He sighed [   ] before he spoke.

The bowl was [   ] placed to show off the flowers.

When she saw the mess, she [   ] brushed it all away.

They all laughed [   ] at the end of the performance.

Reviewing your work

Re-reading, or reviewing, your work is an important part of being a writer. No writer thinks their work is finished without re-reading it and checking it makes sense. Don't worry if you find things that need changing – there are always changes to be made. It is a good opportunity to look at ways in which your writing could be improved.

Here are some ideas to keep in mind when you are reviewing your work.

★ **Make sure your reader will understand your main message.** For example, if you are writing a mystery story, will your reader want to find out what happens? Ask yourself if you have given too many clues to the ending. Is there a feeling of suspense and excitement? If you are writing an explanation, have you used connectives to help the reader follow the process that you are explaining? Would you be able to understand the explanation easily? If you are not sure, have another look at the guidelines for writing explanations.

★ **Make sure you have followed the guidelines for the text type you are writing.** If you are not sure, go back and check. Keep the style constant, and try not to slip from one type of writing to another. If you started in the first person voice, have you kept to it all the way through your writing? Have you kept the same verb tense throughout? Don't get worried if you find mistakes, just correct them and try to remember for the future. No one gets it right all the time, but reviewing your work helps you to spot the errors that could lose you marks.

★ **Check your spelling and grammar.** Look carefully as you read and, if a word doesn't look right, try it out on a piece of paper a few times. If you can, look it up in a dictionary, and try to learn the correct spelling for the future. Read your sentences aloud if you can. This will help you to hear when something doesn't sound right. If you think your grammar is not quite right, try saying the sentence in different ways, and re-write it a few times. Pick the one you think sounds best, and don't be afraid to make changes.

★ **Read as often as you can.** Reading helps you become familiar with good writing, helps you recognise spelling patterns and helps you learn how to structure your sentences. Read as many kinds of books as you can. This will help you to get ideas to use in your own writing.

★ **Keep a notebook and write down ideas, phrases, sentences and words that you like.** If you read a phrase that might be useful, don't be afraid to make use of it. You can learn a lot from other writers' ideas. You never know when they might come in handy.

Handwriting

Handwriting is assessed in your longer writing task so you will need to remember to keep your handwriting neat and easy to read. The maximum you can get for handwriting is 3 marks out of 50.

The Golden Rules

The sections below tell you exactly what you need to do to get the marks, so read these closely. Always remember to follow these golden rules:

- Space out words and sentences evenly.
- Write on the lines if you are using lined paper.
- Use a pencil or pen you feel comfortable with and always use a rubber to rub out mistakes.
- Keep the letters the same size.
- Write so everyone can read your writing!

Getting 1 mark

To get one mark for your handwriting, your writing will need to be legible and be regular in size and spacing.

Getting 2 marks

To get two marks for your handwriting, you will need to:

- keep the handwriting legible;
- write in the correct size and position;
- be flowing and have movement.

Getting 3 marks

To get three marks for your handwriting, you will need to:

- keep the handwriting legible;
- write in the correct size and position;
- be flowing and have movement;
- maintain your own personal style.

★ Tips

- Practise, practise, practise! This is the one way to improve your handwriting. Try to practise a little bit everyday. If you do this in a book you can see how much better your writing is getting.

Notes